Let's Celebrate

MEMORIAL DAY

DISCARD

BY Barbara deRubertis

The Kane Press
New York

For activities and resources for this book and others in the HOLIDAYS & HEROES series, visit: www.kanepress.com/holidays-and-heroes

Text copyright © 2016 by Barbara deRubertis
Photographs/images copyrights: Cover: © Michael Silver Editorial/Alamy; page 1: © JerryPDX/iStock; page 3: © Thomas Arbour/iStock; page 4: © GL Archive/Alamy; pages 5, 6: © North Wind Picture Archives -- All rights reserved; page 7: © Hang Dinh/Shutterstock.com; page 8 top: © Nagel Photography/Shutterstock. com; pages 8–9: Library of Congress, Prints & Photographs Division, LC-DIG-ggbain-13841; page 9 top: Library of Congress, Prints & Photographs Division, LC-DIG-ppmsca-32660; page 10: Courtesy of the author; page 11: © Joseph Sohm/Shutterstock.com; page 12 top: © Artem Kovalenco/Shutterstock.com; page 12 bottom: © Golden Pixels LLC/Shutterstock.com; page 13: © Mindy Schauer/ZUMAPRESS/Newscom; page 14 top: © Neftali/Shutterstock.com; page 14 bottom: © Flo-Bo/Shutterstock.com; page 15: Courtesy of the author; page 16: © MBWTE Photos/Shutterstock.com; page 17: © karenfoleyphotography/iStock; page 18 top: © Sharon Day/Shutterstock.com; page 18 bottom: © Irene Pearcey/Shutterstock.com; page 19 top: © Julie Clopper/Shutterstock.com; page 19 bottom: © Joshua Haviv/Shutterstock.com; page 20 top: © lauradyoung/iStock; page 20 bottom: © Cathleen Abers-Kimball/iStock; page 21: © Aleksander Mirski/iStock; page 22: © Roger L Beltz Gallery; page 23 top: © Hang Dinh/Shutterstock.com; page 23 bottom: Courtesy of the Middle East Conflicts Wall Memorial®; page 24: © PR NEWSWIRE/Newscom; page 25 top: © Tim Evanson; page 25 bottom: © MivPiv/iStock; page 26: © Susan Montgomery/Shutterstock.com; page 27 top: © byvalet/Shutterstock.com; page 27 bottom: © Huguette Roe/Shutterstock.com; page 28: © cdrin/Shutterstock. com; page 29: © Hang Dinh/Shutterstock.com; page 30: © BDphoto/iStock; page 31: © Bob Daemmrich/Alamy; page 32: © Norma Jean Gargasz/Alamy
All due diligence has been conducted in identifying copyright holders and obtaining permissions.

All rights reserved. No part of this book may be reproduced or transmitted in any form or by any means, electronic or mechanical, including photocopying, recording, or by any information storage and retrieval system, without permission in writing from the publisher. For information regarding permission, contact the publisher through its website: www.kanepress.com.

Library of Congress Cataloging-in-Publication Data

deRubertis, Barbara.
 Let's celebrate Memorial Day / by Barbara deRubertis.
    pages cm. -- (Holidays & heroes)
 ISBN 978-1-57565-833-9 (library reinforced binding : alk. paper) -- ISBN 978-1-57565-831-5 (pbk. : alk. paper)
 1. Memorial Day--Juvenile literature. I. Title.
 E642.D52 2016
 394.262--dc23
                                         2015028190

eISBN: 978-1-57565-832-2

1 2 3 4 5 6 7 8 9 10

First published in the United States of America in 2016 by Kane Press, Inc.
Printed in the United States of America

Book Design: Edward Miller
Photograph/Image Research: Poyee Oster

Visit us online at **www.kanepress.com**.

Like us on Facebook
facebook.com/kanepress

Follow us on Twitter
@KanePress

R0446776685

A very special holiday is celebrated on the last Monday in May—Memorial Day. It is the day we honor all the brave men and women in our armed forces who died while fighting to protect our country, our freedoms, and us.

How did this important American holiday come into being?

How Memorial Day Began

From 1861 to 1865, the American Civil War was fought. The northern states did not want to continue allowing slavery, but eleven southern states did. The southern states withdrew from the United States and formed a new country, the Confederate States of America.

President Abraham Lincoln refused to recognize this new country. So the North's Union soldiers and the South's Confederate soldiers went to war.

When the war ended, the United States was "united" again. And slavery would soon be ended. But over half a million soldiers had died fighting on the two sides of the war—far more soldiers than have died in any other American war. The whole country grieved.

Decoration Day

During and after the Civil War, graves of fallen soldiers on both sides were decorated in honor of their sacrifices.

In 1868, General John Logan issued a proclamation: Decoration Day should be held on May 30 every year. He chose that date because flowers would be in bloom and could be used to decorate the graves of all those who died in the Civil War.

A large observance was held that year at Arlington National Cemetery, near Washington, D.C. Speeches were given, followed by people placing flowers on both Union and Confederate graves while singing hymns and saying prayers.

A flowering tree at Arlington National Cemetery

The annual ceremony at Soldiers' National Cemetery in Gettysburg, Pennsylvania, also began in 1868. Gettysburg was the scene of the Civil War's most famous battle: 7,000 soldiers died, more than in any other battle.

Left: Monument at Gettysburg
Below and right: Blue-Gray Reunion, 1913

In July of 1913, veterans of the Union and Confederate armies gathered in Gettysburg to mark the 50-year anniversary of this battle. It was called a "Blue-Gray Reunion" because the Union soldiers' uniforms were blue and the Confederate uniforms were gray. There were speeches, parades, and re-enactments of the battle.

Decoration Day Changes to Memorial Day

"Decoration Day" gradually became known as "Memorial Day," a name first used in 1882.

After the end of the First World War in 1918, the holiday also changed from honoring only those who died in the Civil War. It now honored members of the military who died in *any* American war.

A Memorial Day display of military headwear from different conflicts: Civil War Union Army cap (top); Helmets: First World War (center), Second World War (upper right), Middle East (lower right), Vietnam (lower left), Korea (upper left)

In 1948, members of the Army's 3rd Infantry began a "Flags-In" tradition at Arlington National Cemetery. Just before Memorial Day, they place flags on the graves of all the service members buried there . . . now more than 300,000.

Veterans' groups, Boy Scouts and Girl Scouts, and other groups across America also place flags on service members' graves for this holiday.

Memorial Day became the official name of the holiday in 1967.

National Holiday Act of 1971

In 1971, Congress moved Memorial Day from May 30 to the last Monday in May.

Many people feel this change led to viewing the new three-day weekend as the unofficial beginning of summer. So people often celebrate with picnics and camping trips. Swimming pools open. Stores hold "Memorial Day Sales."

With so much going on, people sometimes forget the real reason for the holiday.

National Moment of Remembrance

In 2000, Congress passed a resolution to help restore the true meaning of Memorial Day. The "National Moment of Remembrance" invites all Americans to stop for a moment of silence at exactly 3:00 P.M. (local time) on Memorial Day. During this moment of silence, we are asked to remember all those who died defending our country's freedoms.

This is one way we can put the "memorial" back in Memorial Day.

Poppies

A Canadian soldier in the First World War was inspired to write the poem "In Flanders Fields" when he saw bright red poppies blooming on the graves of soldiers buried there.

After reading this poem, an American teacher named Moina Michael decided to wear a poppy on Memorial Day to honor those who had died in that war. She sold poppies to her friends and gave the money to help veterans.

Soon afterward, both the American Legion and the Veterans of Foreign Wars began to give away poppies made by disabled veterans. Donations from people receiving the poppies were given to veterans in need of help.

Today the poppies are most often given away on or near Memorial Day and Veterans Day. The poppy has become a symbol of honoring the dead and helping the living.

Memorials for Those Who Died in Wars and Conflicts

Beautiful memorials have been built to honor those who died fighting for our country. It is our way of making sure their sacrifices are not forgotten. And it is comforting for many of the families and friends of those who died to see tributes honoring their loved ones. All of these memorials remind us of our history—and of the price of freedom.

Civil War (1861–1865)

On the anniversary of President Lincoln's most famous speech, the "Gettysburg Address," volunteers in period clothing light candles at Gettysburg National Cemetery. A "luminaria" honors every soldier who died at Gettysburg.

First World War (1917–1918)

The National World War I Museum and Memorial is in Kansas City, Missouri. In 1926, more than 150,000 people gathered to see the Liberty Memorial tower dedicated by President Calvin Coolidge.

Museum exhibits are below the memorial tower and in buildings on either side. At night, steam rises from the top of the tower. Red lights make the steam look like fire!

Second World War (1941–1945)

The World War II Memorial is in Washington, D.C.

A wall containing more than 4,000 Gold Stars pays tribute to the 400,000 Americans who died in this war. Granite columns representing the states and territories form two half-circles around the Rainbow Pool. Two pavilions represent the Atlantic and Pacific fronts on which American forces fought.

Korean Conflict (1950–1953)

The Korean War Veterans Memorial in Washington, D.C., contains a patrol squad—19 stainless steel statues of soldiers walking through a field. A black granite wall displays over 2,400 images of the land, sea, and air troops who supported the foot soldiers.

One part of the granite wall is inscribed "FREEDOM IS NOT FREE."

Vietnam Conflict (1955–1975)

The v-shaped Vietnam Veterans Memorial is also in Washington, D.C. "The Wall" is polished black granite with a mirror-like surface. On it are listed the names of the more than 58,000 Americans who died or went missing in the Vietnam War.

Middle East and Worldwide Conflicts (1979–)

The Middle East Conflicts War Memorial is in Marseilles, Illinois. The wall of granite panels was built to honor the thousands of women and men in our armed forces who have died in worldwide conflicts since 1979. Every year, the names of the women and men who have died during the previous year are etched into the granite slabs right after Memorial Day.

   Family members who visit war memorials often leave medals, flowers, or photos near the names of their loved ones. Each name inscribed on a wall is someone's son or daughter. It may also be someone's sister or brother . . . or husband or wife . . . or mother or father.

   On Memorial Day we remember those who died as well as those who must carry on without them.

The National Memorial Day Concert

The National Memorial Day Concert takes place on the lawn of the United States Capitol Building on the Sunday evening before Memorial Day. Patriotic music is performed, and tribute is paid to the men and women who have given their lives for our country. The concert is broadcast on both radio and television.

The American Veterans Disabled for Life Memorial

In 2015, the National Memorial Day Concert honored not only those who have died but also those who survived with permanent disabilities. The new American Veterans Disabled for Life Memorial is dedicated to these courageous heroes and the challenges they and their families must face every day.

The memorial includes a star-shaped fountain with an eternal flame in the center. Three walls of green glass tell stories of disabled soldiers with their images and their words.

Memorial Day Observances

When the flag is raised on Memorial Day morning, it is first raised to the top of the staff. Then it is slowly lowered to half-staff in honor of the men and women who have given their lives serving our country. At noon, the flag is again raised to full-staff as a reminder that we must continue to defend our freedoms.

The Memorial Day Ceremony at Arlington National Cemetery begins at 11:00 A.M. Flags will have been placed on more than 300,000 graves. A wreath-laying ceremony and concert are held at the Tomb of the Unknown Soldier.

At 12:00 noon the "Rolling Thunder" Motorcycle Rally begins. The thousands of riders who take part are demonstrating their support for improving veteran benefits.

The National Memorial Day Parade begins at 2:00 P.M. in Washington, D.C. In addition to being televised, it is broadcast live to our troops stationed around the world. It includes service members and veterans, service clubs, marching bands, floats, celebrities, and more. It is the largest Memorial Day event in the nation.

There are also thousands of smaller parades and ceremonies held in cities and towns across the United States.

And the National Moment of Remembrance is observed at 3:00 P.M.

Memorial Day and Veterans Day

Two important national holidays honor our women and men in the military.

Memorial Day, on the last Monday in May, honors all those who died while serving in the United States Armed Forces, particularly those who died in battle.

Veterans Day, on November 11, honors *everyone* who has served in the military—both the living and the dead.

Similar events are held on both holidays: parades, ceremonies, concerts, school programs, and poppy distributions. But it is important to remember the difference between the two holidays.

On Memorial Day we think about the more than one million men and women who died defending our country, our freedoms, and us. We feel deeply grateful to every one of them.

Many of us have family members who died defending America and its ideals. On Memorial Day we can share stories about them. We can look at photographs or letters or personal items they left behind. And we can try to imagine how much they loved our country—so much that they were willing to die protecting it.

"Freedom is not free."